EVENT PLANNING SECRETS

The Ultimate Guide to Creating Unforgettable Experiences

AF518080

EVENT PLANNING SECRETS

The Ultimate Guide to Creating Unforgettable Experiences

Sachin Talwar

Worldwide Published by
Pendown Press

PENDOWN PRESS LLP
An ISO 9001 & ISO 14001 Certified Co.,
Regd. Office: 3767A, Kanhaiya Nagar,
Tri Nagar, Delhi-110035
Ph.: 8130886000, 9650072927
E-mail: info@pendownpress.com
Branch Office: 1A/2A, 20, Hari Sadan, Ansari Road,
Daryaganj, New Delhi-110002
Ph.: 011-45794768
Website: PendownPress.com

Edition: 2024
Price: ₹ 499/-
ISBN: 978-93-6338-695-2

All Rights Reserved
All the ideas and thoughts in this book are given by the author and he is responsible for the treatise, facts and dialogues used in this book. He is also responsible for the used pictures and the permission to use them in this book. Copyright of this book is reserved with the author. The publisher does not have any responsibility for the above-mentioned matters. No part of this publication may be reproduced, distributed, or transmitted in any form or by any means, including photocopying, recording, or other electronic or mechanical methods, without the prior written permission of the publisher and author.

Layout and Cover Designed by Pendown Graphics Team
Printed and Bound in India by Thomson Press India Ltd.

To all the amazing event planners,

This book is for you, the heart and soul behind every unforgettable event. Your passion and hard work bring dreams to life and create moments that touch hearts.

This dedication is a tribute to your hard work, your late nights, and your drive to deliver unforgettable experiences.

TABLE OF CONTENTS

Preface

Welcome to a journey through the art and science of event planning. In these pages, you'll find insights that blend creativity with strategy, designed to elevate your events from ordinary to extraordinary.

Event planning is more than just organizing details; it's about crafting unforgettable experiences. Whether you're handling a local gathering or a global conference, the principles and practices shared here will help you create events that resonate deeply with your audience and leave a lasting impression.

This book delves into every aspect of successful event planning—from maximizing your budget and ensuring technical perfection to building strong vendor relationships and engaging a global audience. Each chapter is crafted to provide practical advice and innovative ideas, grounded in real-world experience.

As you read, you'll discover how to manage complex logistics with ease, harness the power of technology, and create an environment that reflects the essence of your brand. With dedicated sections on communication, customization, and strategic planning, this book aims to empower you with the tools and knowledge needed to excel in the dynamic world of event management.

Whether you're an experienced planner or just starting out, my hope is that these insights will inspire and guide you towards creating events that are not only successful but also truly memorable.

Thank you for joining me on this journey. Here's to creating exceptional experiences together.

Warm regards,

Sachin Talwar

❖ ❖ ❖

Introduction

Want your event to be the talk of the town?

It's time to make your event the one everyone's talking about. With years of experience and know-how from planning over 3,500 events, this book is your backstage pass to creating events that are nothing short of spectacular.

Get Ready to Unlock the Secrets Behind Award-Winning Events

- Master Customization for Lasting Impressions
- Discover Innovative Creative Concepts
- Achieve Technical Perfection in Every Detail
- Engage and Inspire Your Audience
- Manage Budgets Without Cutting Corners
- Handle Global Audiences Seamlessly

This book isn't just about planning good events. It's about creating amazing, unforgettable experiences.

Prepare to stand out. Prepare to inspire. Prepare to redefine what's possible. Your journey to event greatness starts here.

❖ ❖ ❖

Know Your Author

Sachin Talwar, a true visionary in the world of event management, has dedicated over two decades to crafting extraordinary experiences. His journey began as a backstage enthusiast at MTV's Video Gaga contest and has evolved into leading WOW Events, a testament to his relentless passion and commitment.

Since founding WOW Events in 2008, Sachin has orchestrated over 3,500 events for more than 200 global brands, each one reflecting his meticulous attention to detail and profound understanding of client visions. His exceptional work has earned WOW Events prestigious accolades, including EEMAX Gold and Silver awards.

Sachin's approach goes beyond the surface. He believes in creating events that resonate deeply with audiences, blending customization, innovation, and flawless execution into every project. His global perspective is evident in his successful execution of events across 19 countries, showcasing his ability to adapt to diverse cultures and preferences.

His journey is not just about the glitz and glamour but about making a meaningful impact through every event, ensuring each one leaves an unforgettable impression.

Acknowledgement

Dear Readers,

I am grateful for the opportunity to share my experiences and insights with you. This book represents a compilation of years of experience, learning, and growth. I hope that the words within these pages inspire, inform, and resonate with each reader.

I am deeply grateful to the wonderful individuals who have played instrumental roles in shaping my journey and contributing to my achievements.

My wife, Roopali, you are not just my partner but the foundation of my strength. I couldn't have done this without your love and patience.

Aumav, Namaah, and Shivaay, my wonderful children, your laughter and joy infuse my days with purpose and motivation. You inspire me to reach for the stars.

My brother and co-founder, Amit, who stood with me on this journey like a rock, your passion for execution has given wings to my imagination.

To my mentors and friends, your guidance and wisdom have shaped me into the person I am today. I owe much of my success to your invaluable mentorship.

To all mentioned and those not named, your contributions have been crucial to my journey. Together, we have built something extraordinary, and I look forward to the continued journey of growth and success with each one of you.

Thank you for being a part of this shared experience.

❖ ❖ ❖

Why This Book?

This book shows you how to take your event planning to the next level. By using these tips and strategies, you'll create amazing events that impress and engage your audience. You'll see better results and set yourself apart in the event planning world.

Let's not wait any longer—start exploring a new perspective on event management today!

Chapter 1

Discover the Secret Behind Award-Winning Event Planners

> *"Success is no accident. It is hard work, perseverance, learning, studying, sacrifice, and, most of all, love of what you are doing or learning to do."*
>
> **- Pelé**

Ever wondered what sets award-winning event planners apart from the rest? It's not just about having a flashy website, fancy decorations, a star-studded guest list or a big team. The secret lies in their experience, dedication, and a keen eye for detail.

Award-winning event planners have a proven track record. They have successfully executed numerous events, from corporate conferences to grand product launches. Their accolades, such as EEMAX Gold & Silver awards, really show what they're capable of. These awards are given to those who excel in creating impactful and memorable events.

For example, consider a company that organizes an annual dealer conference for a major brand like UltraTech Cement. An award-winning event planner would ensure every detail, from the venue to the stage setup, aligns perfectly with the brand's image. They would also have backup plans for any unexpected issues, making sure that everything runs smoothly.

Such planners also emphasize client testimonials. Positive feedback from previous clients builds trust and showcases their ability to deliver outstanding events. When choosing an event planner, look for these testimonials and awards. They're indicators of quality and reliability. And let's not forget the power of word-of-mouth. These planners have a loyal following of clients who rave about their ability to turn dreams into reality.

So, when you're searching for the perfect partner to bring your vision to life, look for these qualities: experience, awards, and client feedback. These factors ensure your event will be in capable hands, leading to a successful and memorable experience for all attendees. It's a winning combination that guarantees an event that will be talked about for years to come.

❖ ❖ ❖

Chapter 2

How to Make Your Event Unforgettable with Customization

> *"To be yourself in a world that is constantly trying to make you something else is the greatest accomplishment."*
>
> **– Ralph Waldo Emerson**

In a world saturated with events, standing out requires more than just a grand scale or star power. It demands a deep understanding of your audience and a commitment to tailoring the experience to their unique preferences. This is where customization shines.

Imagine attending an event where every detail resonates with your interests. It's an exhilarating experience that leaves a lasting impression. Customization is the art of creating this kind of connection. By putting your audience at the heart of your event planning, you can transform a simple gathering into a truly unforgettable experience.

1. Understanding Your Audience

The first step to customization is to delve deep into your audience's world. Who are they? What are their passions, values, and expectations? By conducting thorough audience research, you gain invaluable insights that guide your decision-making process. For instance, a tech conference filled with interactive workshops and cutting-edge demonstrations would thrill a tech-savvy audience, while a laid-back outdoor setting with live music might be perfect for a family-friendly picnic.

2. Crafting a Customized Theme

A strong theme provides the backbone for your event. But it's not enough to choose a theme; it must align with your audience and brand identity. For example, if your brand is known for innovation, a futuristic theme with cutting-edge design elements can reinforce this image.

3. Personalized Touches

Personalized touches make a big difference. Consider customized invitations, personalized name badges, and tailored giveaways. These small details show that you value your attendees and have put thought into making the event special for them.

Interactive elements are also crucial. Engage your audience with activities, workshops, or live polls. This involvement makes them feel like an integral part of the event, rather than passive observers. This not only boosts engagement but also creates opportunities for networking and knowledge sharing.

4. The Power of Follow-Up

The journey doesn't end when the event concludes. A well-crafted follow-up campaign can solidify your event's impact. Personalized thank-you notes, exclusive offers, or invitations to future events show that you value your attendees' participation and create opportunities for long-term relationships.

In conclusion, customization is about making your event unique and relevant to your audience. It's about creating an experience that resonates with your audience on a personal level, leaving them with memories that will last a lifetime. So, dare to be different, and let customization be the secret ingredient that transforms your event into an unforgettable success.

Chapter 3

Unlock the Power of Creative Concepts for Your Brand

> *"Creativity is intelligence having fun."*
>
> ***– Albert Einstein***

Creative concepts are the backbone of any memorable event. They not only set the tone but also create a unique experience that resonates with attendees long after the event ends. Your brand is the foundation upon which your creative concept should be built. By understanding your brand's essence, values, and target audience, you can develop ideas that resonate authentically. So, how do you unlock this power for your brand?

Start by brainstorming ideas that align with your brand's identity. For instance, if your brand is known for sustainability, consider an eco-friendly event theme. This could include using recycled materials for decorations, offering plant-based catering, and encouraging attendees to carpool or use public transport.

Another approach is to incorporate storytelling. Humans are wired for stories. Create a narrative around your event that engages and excites your audience. For example, a tech company might host an event themed around the future of innovation, with each segment telling a part of the story about upcoming technological advancements.

Interactive elements can also enhance your creative concept. Think about incorporating virtual reality experiences, interactive workshops, or live demonstrations. These elements not only captivate your audience but also encourage active participation, making the event more memorable.

Don't forget about the power of visuals. Stunning graphics, vibrant colors, and creative stage designs can leave a lasting impression. For instance, a healthcare company could use calming blue and green hues and nature-inspired designs to create a serene and healing atmosphere.

Lastly, consider the overall experience. How do you want your attendees to feel? Excited, inspired, relaxed? Tailor your event elements to evoke these emotions. For example, a fitness brand might create an energizing atmosphere with upbeat music, dynamic lighting, and fitness challenges.

In summary, unlocking the power of creative concepts involves aligning your ideas with your brand's identity, incorporating storytelling, using interactive elements, focusing on visuals, and tailoring the overall experience to evoke desired emotions. This approach ensures your event is not just attended but remembered.

❖ ❖ ❖

Chapter 4

Is Your Event Technically Flawless? Here's What You Might Be Missing

> *"Details create the big picture."*
>
> ***– Sanford I. Weill***

A technically flawless event can make a world of difference in creating a seamless and enjoyable experience for attendees. But achieving this perfection requires meticulous planning and attention to detail.

1. Right AV Equipment

First, ensure you have the right AV equipment. This includes high-quality microphones, speakers, projectors, and LED screens. For example, during a corporate presentation, clear audio and sharp visuals are crucial. Test all equipment beforehand to avoid any glitches.

- **Pro Tip:** Have a dedicated AV team on hand to handle any technical issues that may arise during the event.

2. Stage Setup

Next, think about the stage setup. Proper lighting can enhance the mood and focus attention where it's needed. For instance, spotlights on the speaker can keep the audience engaged during a keynote address. Additionally, consider using dynamic lighting effects for entertainment segments to add excitement.

➢ **Pro Tip:** Use LED lighting for energy efficiency and better control over lighting effects.

3. Internet Connectivity

Another critical aspect is internet connectivity. Reliable Wi-Fi is essential, especially for live streaming or interactive elements like audience polls. Make sure the venue has sufficient bandwidth to accommodate all attendees.

➢ **Pro Tip:** Set up a dedicated network for presenters and critical event staff to ensure uninterrupted connectivity.

4. Backup Plans

Don't overlook the importance of a backup plan. Technical issues can arise unexpectedly, so having backup equipment and technical support on standby is vital. For instance, if a microphone fails during a speech, a quick switch to a backup can save the moment.

➢ **Pro Tip:** Conduct a risk assessment to identify potential technical failures and prepare contingency plans accordingly.

5. Event Management Software

Also, consider integrating event management software. Tools for registration, scheduling, and communication can streamline the event process and enhance the attendee experience. For example, a mobile app with the event schedule, speaker bios, and real-time updates can keep everyone informed and engaged.

- **Pro Tip:** Choose software that offers analytics to gain insights into attendee engagement and event performance.

6. Thorough Rehearsals

Rehearse thoroughly. A full run-through with all technical elements in place can help identify potential issues and ensure everyone knows their role. This practice can make the actual event run smoothly and confidently.

- **Pro Tip:** Schedule multiple rehearsals, including a dress rehearsal with all speakers and performers present.

In conclusion, a technically flawless event requires careful planning, high-quality equipment, reliable connectivity, backup plans, effective event management tools, and thorough rehearsals. By focusing on these elements, you can ensure your event runs without a hitch.

❖ ❖ ❖

Chapter 5

The Stress-Free Event Planning Hack You Need to Know

> *"The key is not to prioritize what's on your schedule, but to schedule your priorities."*
>
> **– Stephen Covey**

Event planning can be stressful, but with the right approach, you can make the process much smoother and more enjoyable. Here's the ultimate hack: Effective Project Management.

Start by breaking down the event planning process into manageable tasks. Create a detailed checklist that covers every aspect of the event, from initial planning to post-event follow-up. For example, your checklist might include tasks like venue selection, catering arrangements, speaker coordination, and marketing.

Next, set clear deadlines for each task. This helps you stay on track and ensures that nothing is left to the last minute. For instance, if your event is in six months, you might set a deadline for finalizing the venue within the first month.

Use project management tools to keep everything organized. Platforms like Trello or Asana allow you to create task boards, assign responsibilities, and track progress. For example, you can create a board for your event with columns for each planning stage, such as "To Do," "In Progress," and "Completed" to visualize your planning stages.

Effective communication is also crucial. Regular check-ins with your team can help identify any issues early and keep everyone on the same page. For instance, a weekly meeting to discuss progress and address concerns can prevent last-minute surprises.

Delegate tasks to trusted team members. Trying to do everything yourself can lead to burnout and mistakes. Assign specific roles to team members based on their strengths. For example, if someone excels at social media, let them handle the event's online promotion.

Lastly, don't forget to take care of yourself. Event planning can be demanding, so ensure you're getting enough rest and taking breaks when needed. A clear mind is essential for effective planning and decision-making.

In conclusion, the key to stress-free event planning hack is effective project management. By breaking tasks down, setting deadlines, using tools, communicating effectively, delegating tasks, and taking care of yourself, you can plan a successful event without the stress.

❖ ❖ ❖

Chapter 6

Why Vendor Relationships Can Make or Break Your Event

> *"Alone we can do so little;*
> *together we can do so much."*
>
> ***– Helen Keller***

Strong vendor relationships are crucial for the success of any event. Vendors are the backbone of any successful event, from the caterers and decorators to the AV technicians and transportation providers. Building and maintaining strong vendor relationships can significantly impact the success of your event. Reliable vendors ensure that everything from catering to AV equipment is top-notch, making your event run smoothly and impressively. Here's why these relationships are so important and how to make the most of them.

1. Reliability and Trust

Firstly, good vendor relationships mean you can count on quality, trust, and reliability. When you work with vendors you have a good relationship with, you can count on them to deliver high-quality services and products. This trust is essential for ensuring that every aspect of your event runs smoothly. For example, if your caterer understands your expectations and has a history of reliability, you can be confident that your guests will enjoy a delicious meal without any last-minute issues. A reliable AV vendor means the technical aspects of your event, like sound and visuals, will work flawlessly.

2. Sourcing Vendors

Building these relationships takes time and effort. Start by researching and choosing vendors with excellent reputations. Look for reviews, ask for references, and check their previous work to assess their reliability and quality. Consider attending industry events or seeking recommendations from other event planners. Once you find potential vendors, meet with them to discuss your needs and expectations.

3. Communication

Communication is key. Keep an open line of communication with your vendors throughout the planning process. Regular check-ins and updates can help prevent misunderstandings and ensure everyone is on the same page. For instance, if you need a specific type of lighting setup, clearly convey your requirements and confirm that the vendor can deliver.

4. Flexibility and Problem-Solving

Events rarely go exactly as planned, and having vendors who are flexible and adept at problem-solving can make a huge difference. Vendors you've worked with before are more likely to accommodate last-minute changes or special requests. For example, if you need to adjust the menu due to dietary restrictions, a good relationship with your caterer can make this change seamless.

5. Going the Extra Mile

Additionally, reliable vendors often go above and beyond to ensure your event's success. They might offer suggestions based on their experience or provide extra services at no additional cost. For example, an AV vendor might recommend the best sound setup for your venue or include additional equipment for better coverage.

Vendor relationships can truly make or break your event. By choosing reputable vendors, maintaining clear communication, and fostering flexibility, you can ensure your event runs smoothly and impresses your attendees.

❖ ❖ ❖

Chapter 7

The Key to Maximum Attendee Engagement at Your Next Event

> *"Tell me and I forget. Teach me and I remember. Involve me and I learn."*
>
> ***– Benjamin Franklin***

Engaging your attendees is crucial for the success of any event. When attendees are actively involved, they're more likely to remember the experience and associate positive feelings with your brand. Here are some secrets to achieving maximum engagement at your next event.

1. Understand Your Audience

The first step in maximizing attendee engagement is to deeply understand your audience. Knowing their interests, preferences, and needs allows you to tailor your event to their expectations. Conduct surveys or interviews, analyze past event feedback, and research industry trends to gather insights. For example, if you're organizing a tech conference, understanding that your audience values hands-on experiences with new technologies can guide your planning process.

2. Interactive Content and Formats

One effective way to boost engagement is through interactive activities. These can range from live polls and Q&A sessions to hands-on workshops and demonstrations. For example, at a tech conference, you could have a demo area where attendees can try out the latest gadgets.

3. Gamification

Gamification is another powerful tool. Incorporate games and challenges into your event to make it more fun and engaging. For instance, you could have a scavenger hunt where attendees collect points by visiting different booths or participating in activities. The winner could receive a prize, adding an element of competition.

4. Networking Opportunities

Networking opportunities are also important. Create spaces and activities that encourage attendees to connect with each other. For example, a networking lounge or speed networking sessions can facilitate meaningful interactions. Providing a mobile app where attendees can view profiles and schedule meetings can also enhance networking.

5. Engaging Speakers and Presenters

The quality of your speakers and presenters plays a significant role in engagement. Choose speakers who are not only knowledgeable but also dynamic and engaging. Encourage them to use storytelling techniques, interactive demonstrations, and multimedia to keep the audience interested. For instance, a presenter who uses compelling case studies and engaging visuals will likely hold the audience's attention better than one who relies solely on text-heavy slides.

6. Technology

Incorporating technology can also boost engagement. Use event apps to keep attendees informed and involved. Features like live updates, interactive maps, and social media integration can enhance the overall experience. For example, a live poll during a keynote speech can make attendees feel like their opinions matter.

7. Live Entertainment and Activities

Include live entertainment and activities to add energy and excitement to your event. Music performances, live demonstrations, or interactive workshops can break up the monotony of traditional sessions and keep attendees engaged. For example, a live band or a cooking demonstration can offer a refreshing change of pace and provide entertainment between sessions.

Remember, engagement is a two-way street. By involving your attendees, you create a memorable experience that strengthens your brand and builds lasting relationships. In conclusion, maximizing attendee engagement involves interactive activities, gamification, networking opportunities, personalization, technology integration, and dynamic content. So, let your creativity run wild and watch your event come to life.

❖ ❖ ❖

Chapter 8

What Happens After the Event? The Importance of Post-Event Analysis

> *"Success is the sum of details."*
>
> ***– Harvey S. Firestone***

The event might be over, but the work doesn't stop there. Post-event analysis is crucial for understanding the success of your event and identifying areas for improvement.

Start by gathering feedback from attendees. Surveys are a great tool for this. Send out a questionnaire asking about their overall experience, what they enjoyed, and what could be improved. For example, you could ask about the quality of the speakers, the relevance of the content, and the effectiveness of the networking opportunities.

Next, analyze the event data. Look at metrics such as attendance numbers, social media engagement, and app usage. For instance, if your event had a mobile app, check how many attendees used it, which features were most popular, and any comments or reviews left by users.

Review your goals and objectives. Compare your actual outcomes with your initial goals. Did you achieve what you set out to do? For example, if your goal was to increase brand awareness, look at the reach and engagement of your event's social media posts and any media coverage.

Meet with your team and vendors to discuss what went well and what didn't. An open and honest debrief can provide valuable insights. For instance, if there were technical issues, discuss how they were handled and what can be done to prevent them in the future.

Document your findings in a post-event report. This report should include attendee feedback, data analysis, goal review, and team debrief notes. For example, if attendees loved a particular speaker, make a note to invite them back for future events. If there were issues with the venue, consider alternatives for next time.

Finally, use these insights to plan your next event. Continuous improvement is key to event success. By learning from each event, you can make the next one even better.

In conclusion, post-event analysis is essential for measuring success and identifying areas for improvement. By gathering feedback, analyzing data, reviewing goals, debriefing with your team, and documenting findings, you can ensure continuous improvement for future events.

❖ ❖ ❖

Chapter 9

How to Maximize Your Event Budget Without Cutting Corners

> *"A budget is telling your money where to go instead of wondering where it went."*
>
> ***– Dave Ramsey***

Maximizing your event budget without compromising on quality is a challenge, but it's definitely achievable with careful planning and smart strategies.

Start by setting clear priorities. Determine what aspects of the event are most important and allocate your budget accordingly. For example, if a high-quality sound system is crucial for your event, allocate more funds there and look for savings elsewhere.

- **Pro Tip:** Use a digital survey tool to gather input from team members or stakeholders on which aspects of the event they believe should be prioritized.

Negotiate with vendors. Building strong relationships with vendors can lead to better deals and discounts. For instance, if you've worked with a caterer before, they might offer you a loyalty discount. Don't be afraid to ask for discounts or negotiate better terms.

- **Pro Tip:** Develop strong negotiation skills to secure the best possible deals with vendors, venues, and service providers.

Consider off-peak times. Hosting your event during less busy times can result in significant savings. For example, venues and vendors might offer lower rates during weekdays or off-season months.

- **Pro Tip:** Use a collaborative calendar tool to visualize potential event dates and compare pricing for different time slots with your team.

Be resourceful with your resources. Use what you already have or can borrow. For instance, if you have access to quality photography equipment, use that instead of hiring a professional photographer. Similarly, leverage in-house talent for tasks like graphic design or social media management.

- **Pro Tip:** Create a shared document where team members can list available resources and skills, and collaborate on how to best utilize them for the event.

Plan for contingencies. Set aside a portion of your budget for unexpected expenses. This way, you're not caught off guard by last-minute costs. For example, if you have a 10 % contingency fund, you'll be better prepared for unforeseen issues like extra transportation costs or additional equipment rental.

- **Pro Tip:** Use a budgeting tool that includes a contingency planning feature to model different scenarios and allocate resources accordingly.

Look for sponsorship opportunities. Partnering with sponsors can significantly offset costs. For example, a tech company might sponsor the AV equipment in exchange for branding opportunities. This not only saves money but also adds value to your event.

- **Pro Tip:** Create an interactive sponsorship proposal template that allows for easy customization and collaboration with your team to attract and secure sponsors.

Evaluate and track your expenses closely. Use budget tracking tools to monitor your spending and ensure you're staying within your limits. For example, spreadsheets or specialized event budgeting software can help you keep track of every expense.

- **Pro Tip:** Set up a shared budget tracking spreadsheet or software where team members can input and update expenses in real time, allowing for transparent and collaborative budget management.

In summary, maximizing your event budget involves setting clear priorities, negotiating with vendors, considering off-peak times, being resourceful, planning for contingencies, seeking sponsorships, and closely tracking expenses. By following these strategies, you can create a successful event without cutting corners.

❖ ❖ ❖

Chapter 10

Can Your Event Company Handle a Global Audience? Find Out Here

> *"To handle yourself, use your head;*
> *to handle others, use your heart."*
>
> ***– Eleanor Roosevelt***

Handling a global audience requires more than just scaling up your event. It involves careful planning, cultural sensitivity, and robust logistics to ensure a seamless experience for all attendees.

First, consider the cultural diversity of your audience. Understanding cultural nuances is crucial. For example, accommodating dietary restrictions, language preferences, and cultural holidays in your event planning can make a significant difference. Offering translations or interpreters can also make your event more accessible. Additionally, include cultural elements in your event, such as region-specific entertainment or cuisine, to make it more engaging for diverse attendees.

Next, think about time zones. Scheduling sessions that accommodate different time zones ensures that more attendees can participate. For example, if your event is global, you might need to schedule keynotes at times that are convenient for both Asian and American attendees. Provide recorded sessions for those who cannot attend live, ensuring they don't miss out on valuable content.

Technology plays a significant role in reaching a global audience. Ensure you have reliable and high-quality live streaming services. For example, using platforms like Zoom or Microsoft Teams can help you host webinars and virtual conferences efficiently. Test these technologies thoroughly to avoid technical glitches, and have technical support available during the event to address any issues promptly.

Logistics are another critical factor. If your event has physical elements, such as shipped materials or localized hubs, ensure timely delivery and coordination. For instance, if you're sending out welcome kits to attendees, plan for shipping times to different regions. Coordinate with local partners to streamline these processes and avoid delays.

Communication is key. Keep your global audience informed with clear and regular updates. Use multiple channels, such as emails, social media, and your event app, to ensure everyone receives important information. For example, send reminders about session times and provide clear instructions for joining virtual events. Consider setting up a dedicated global support team to assist attendees from different regions.

Lastly, gather feedback from your global attendees. Understand their experiences and identify any challenges they faced. This feedback can help you improve future events. For example, if attendees from Europe faced difficulties with session timings, you can adjust your schedule for the next event. Use feedback surveys and conduct follow-up interviews to collect detailed insights.

In conclusion, handling a global audience involves understanding cultural diversity, accommodating different time zones, leveraging technology, managing logistics, maintaining clear communication, and gathering feedback. By focusing on these aspects, your event company can successfully host events that resonate with a global audience and create a truly memorable experience.

❖ ❖ ❖

Connect, Collaborate, and Create!

Your journey to extraordinary events starts here.

Thank you for taking the time to read this book. I hope you found it both enjoyable and informative. If you have any questions or if you'd like to connect personally to elevate your event planning to the next level, I would be delighted to help.

Ready to turn your vision into reality? Let's connect. I'd love to hear about your event vision and explore how we can bring it to life together.

Sachin Talwar

+91 9958634635

sachin@wowevents.in

WOW Events Pvt Ltd

1/7, 3rd Floor, East Patel Nagar

New Delhi – 110008 India